Table Time Trouble

Story by Amber R. Carter

Illustrations by Lowell Hildebrandt

2021 Book Club
Local Artist
Amber Carter

AuthorHouse™
1663 Liberty Drive
Bloomington, IN 47403
www.authorhouse.com
Phone: 1-800-839-8640

©2009 Amber R. Carter. All rights reserved.

No part of this book may be reproduced, stored in a retrieval system, or transmitted by any means without the written permission of the author.

First published by AuthorHouse 11/18/2009

ISBN: 978-1-4389-6025-8 (sc)

Printed in the United States of America
Bloomington, Indiana

This book is printed on acid-free paper.

To my husband and children who inspired the story as the real table time trouble crew. To my neighbor, Laura Coor, for her help discovering the new names of the kids, Dr. Kevin Fedak and Karen Fedak for giving me a vision of Dr. Mindyourmanners and my good friend Carolyn Logue for her help with editing.

-God Bless

"Would you look at the way they eat?" said the mother to the father.

"Its horrible." he replied. "I wish there was something we could do about it."

The father and mother had four children, a girl and three boys. The children were good kids but there was one problem. They had very bad table manners. So bad, the parents had to warn everyone they met. The parents warned people for so long that soon these warnings became new names for the children.

The girl was the oldest and her name was Miss Elbows O'Hair. Miss Elbows O'Hair had very long hair and loved to play with it. Miss Elbows O'Hair always put her elbows on the table. The type of table did not matter, short tables and tall tables, coffee tables and pool tables. When Miss Elbows O'Hair saw a table, she placed her elbows firmly on the table and twirled her hair. This was a real problem when it was time to eat. Elbows on the table and twirl, twirl, twirl. Her hair flew everywhere. With so much hair flying around, the parents worried a hairball would stick in her throat and make their daughter choke. There was hair in the air, hair on the table, and hair in the food. Gross. Icky. Yuck. Nobody wants hair in their food, nobody.

This was very true for the youngest child, Mister Finicky. This boy would never eat food with hair in it. Mr. Finicky was the most finicky person ever. Everything had to be just so and in its proper place. The food he ate had a very particular taste. He had ketchup on eggs and macaroni and cheese without any lumps please. Took the crust off his bread and peeled the grapes. Added chips to his creamy peanut butter sandwich. Made sure it was not too creamy or too crunchy. He did not let his food touch anything else. If it did, Mister Finicky did not eat it. If the food was not the right texture, temperature or color, Mister Finicky did not eat it. With all the complaining and picking at his food, the poor parents worried about his health and if he was getting enough vitamins.

Sir Talksalot, the next boy, could tell you all about it. Sir Talksalot was very tall and slender and talked a lot. People rarely saw him eat, because all he did was talk. This boy really talked. He liked mealtime because when everyone else started eating, he told stories. Sir Talksalot loved it. He talked and everyone had to listen to him. It was brilliant! Even after everyone was gone from the table, Sir Talksalot kept talking. Story after story, after story. Talk, talk, talk. The parents worried that he did not eat enough food. Between stories, they tried to put food in his mouth, but Sir Talksalot talked too fast. They tried to get his attention but he did not hear them because, well, because he talked a lot and because of the noise from the last child. Hoverandshovel.

Hoverandshovel made so much noise when he ate that you could barely hear the stories of Sir Talksalot. Hoverandshovel did not put his elbows on the table, twirl his hair, or talk while he was supposed to be eating. No, he did not have any of these problems. He ate well and unlike Mister Finicky, he ate all his food, all the leftovers and anything else he could get his hands on. Yes, he was a very good eater. His problem was that he was too good! He hovered over his plate and started shoveling the food in. You had to watch out when Hoverandshovel started eating because he was very messy! The food would make a squishy, scrunchy noise with an occasional slurp. The food flew from his mouth between bites because he was shoveling it in so fast. He ate so fast, he did not know what he was eating or what it tasted like. The worried parents wondered if Hoverandshovel would ever get full or if he would become supersized like his appetite.

These were the children and the parents did not know what to do.

"Elbows off the table and stop playing with your hair" the mother told Miss Elbows O'Hair.

"Eat your food and don't complain." the father exclaimed to Mister Finicky.

"Stop talking and eat faster." the mother yelled to Sir Talksalot.

The father said, "Slow down and chew your food" to Hoverandshovel.

The children did not listen. They kept eating with horrible table manners. Twirl, twirl, twirl. Complain, complain, complain. Talk, talk, talk. Spray, spray, spray. Hair and food flew everywhere. Oh what a mess! The parents had to do something fast. The mother tried to get their attention with no luck. Finally the father said, "You kids better behave at the table or Doctor Mindyourmanners is going to find you!" However, the children did not hear him over the noise of their eating. Day after day, the parents had the same problem at meals. Table time was trouble.

One day, the kids were at the table eating with their very bad table manners when the doorbell rang. The mother went to answer the door.

What happened next was quite bizarre, absolutely amazing and will make you think carefully about how you eat your next meal.

Instead of their mother returning, an odd-looking person walked over to the table. He looked like a mad scientist with crazy silver hair, dark rimmed glasses and a white lab coat. A strange light was strapped on his head and he carried a notepad with a really big pencil. The man walked around the table and looked at each child very carefully while they ate. "Hmmm. I see. Terrible. This is going to be challenging," he said.

"Who are you? What is your name? What is that notepad for and where is our mother?" asked Sir Talksalot.

"Let me introduce myself. My name is Doctor Mindyourmanners, the notepad is for taking notes and your mother is taking a much needed break."

"What are you doing here?" asked Sir Talksalot.

"Oh you shall see that soon enough. Please, continue eating while I finish taking notes." Doctor Mindyourmanners said.

The kids went back to eating. Miss Elbows O'Hair placed her elbows back on the table and started twirling her hair while eating her food. Soon hair was everywhere. Mister Finicky complained about the lumps in his macaroni and cheese while Sir Talksalot started a new story about his greatest adventure ever. Hoverandshovel was simply a blur of flying food as he shoveled it into his mouth.

Doctor Mindyourmanners had seen enough.

"Excuse me, I'll be right back," he said.

The children were puzzled but continued twirling, talking, complaining and shoveling.

All of a sudden, there was a loud noise from the other room and the doctor yelled, "Got it." Then they heard another noise and the doctor said "This will work." and "Just what I need." The kids were even more puzzled but kept on with their bad table manners.

Soon Doctor Mindyourmanners came back to the table carrying a bag full of funny looking contraptions.

"What is going on?" asked Miss Elbows O'Hair.

Doctor Mindyourmanners replied, "I am glad you asked. If you would be so kind as to stand up and hold out your hands please, I will show you the first of the manners machines."

Miss Elbows O'Hair was very curious so she quickly stood up. Doctor Mindyourmanners looked at Miss Elbows O'Hair and explained, "Your elbows must come off the table and your hair needs to stay out of everybody's food. The solution for you is a Ponylet Chair. This new chair has no arms, legs or seat. It is more like a bracelet for your arms connected to a ponytail holder for your hair."

Before Miss Elbows O'Hair knew what was happening, Doctor Mindyourmanners put her in the Ponylet Chair. Both hands were in a bracelet holding her hair behind her head and away from the food.

"How am I supposed to finish my food?" asked Miss Elbows O'Hair.

"Hmm, we will have to see," replied Doctor Mindyourmanners. "This is a new device and I appreciate you testing it for me."

Sir Talksalot thought that was funny and began to talk about how funny it was. However, before he could finish his story, Doctor Mindyourmanners was by his side with another manners machine.

Sir Talksalot became very excited and asked, "Is that for me? What is it? Can I touch it?"

Doctor Mindyourmanners replied, "Yes, this is for you. It is a Food Funnel. Please hold still while I put it on your head." Sir Talksalot frowned and began to talk but the doctor put the Food Funnel on his face muffling all of his words.

The Doctor told Sir Talksalot, "This Food Funnel is finely tuned to process food with flavor and fun. When it stops, you can talk but then and only then. So eat your food timely and choose your words wisely."

Hoverandshovel thought the Food Funnel was the most amazing thing he had ever seen. He was hoping Doctor Mindyourmanners would give him a Food Funnel so he could eat food even faster. Quickly Hoverandshovel asked, "What about me? Can I have a Food Funnel too? Pretty please with whip cream and a cherry on top?" he asked hungrily.

Doctor Mindyourmanners replied sweetly, "No, I have something even better in mind for you." The doctor reached in his bag and said, "Come here and take a look."

Hoverandshovel froze when he saw what Doctor Mindyourmanners was holding.

"A miniature fork and spoon!" yelled Hoverandshovel. How am I supposed to eat with that?"

"Hoverandshovel, you eat too fast and must slow down to appreciate your food. Use this miniature set very carefully and your food will taste quite wonderful." said Doctor Mindyourmanners with a smile.

By now, Mister Finicky was very worried about what kind of manners machine Doctor Mindyourmanners had in store for him. He tried to leave the room quietly while nobody was looking when the doctor saw him.

"Don't go away yet" said Doctor Mindyourmanners. "I have a very special manners machine for you too."

"That's what I was afraid of!" gulped Mister Finicky.

"Here is your manners machine. Give it a try. It is a Super Food Shake machine to blend, squish and liquefy."

Mister Finicky looked at his Super Food Shake machine and asked, "How will I keep my food from touching other food?"

"You must learn to stop complaining and appreciate the food that you are given." Doctor Mindyourmanners quickly replied.

All of the children were quite surprised that they would have to eat their food a new way. Doctor Mindyourmanners put the bad table manners to a test that day.

Miss Elbows O'Hair could not twirl her hair because she had no place for her elbows to go with her new Ponylet Chair. Instead of hair flying everywhere and landing in the food, the hair of Miss Elbows O'Hair stayed on her head and all was good.

Without a word, the Food Funnel started to work and Sir Talksalot realized he was actually hungry. Instead of telling another story just to hear his voice, he heard a different sound he had never heard before, a grumbling in his tummy. It started softly and grew louder until Sir Talksalot had the Food Funnel working full throttle. Occasionally, the Food Funnel would stop to allow Sir Talksalot to talk just a little and then he would continue his meal.

Mr. Finicky had his first Food Shake. Hot food mixed with cold, sweet foods mixed with sour. The Food Shake mixed everything together and left lumps everywhere. He did not know what to complain about first so he shrugged his shoulders, plugged his nose and said "Down the hatch." After his first drink, he realized the blend of foods created a wonderful new taste so he ate his food shake without a complaint.

Hoverandshovel had it tough with his miniature plate and silverware set. At first, he was so frustrated he stabbed at the miniature plate like a giant. Finally, he slowed down so he would not miss the food on the miniature plate with his miniature fork and spoon. He took longer between bites and this made him notice the food. Everything had a flavor and smell that he never noticed before.

Doctor Mindyourmanners said to the children, "My job is done here and now I must be on my way. Your new table manners will make your parents very happy. Before the kids could say good-bye, Doctor Mindyourmanners was gone.

Soon, the mother and father came home and saw the children eating. They were used to seeing food flying in the air as Hoverandshovel ate or bits of hair moving from plate to plate as Miss Elbows O'Hair played with her hair with her elbows on the table. The mother expected Mister Finicky to complain and thought she would have to ask Sir Talksalot to stop talking so much. Instead, the table was quiet and calm as the kids ate their lunch. The parents laughed and smiled. They were very pleased.

Soon the mother said, "I can't call you Miss Elbows O'Hair, Mister Finicky, Sir Talksalot and Hoverandshovel anymore."

The kids stopped eating and looked at each other. Their table manners had been bad for so long they had forgotten their real names. "What are our real names?" they asked.

The father replied, "Your elbows are off the table and you are not twirling your hair, Ellen."

He laughed and looked at the former Mister Finicky and said, "Your Food Shake has fixed your finickiness," Fred.

The mother was quite happy when she told Hoverandshovel that his real name is Henry.

She then turned to Sir Talksalot and slyly said, "Your stories were long but your name is simple and short. It's Bob."

The children learned to mind their manners at the table that day. Table time was not trouble any more. The parents looked forward to table time with their children instead of wondering what or how they were eating! They did not have to worry about who would eat what or if hair would land in their food. Stories were told, but everyone had a chance to talk.

So, before you use bad table manners like complaining about your food, chewing with your mouth open or putting your elbows on the table, remember this story. Otherwise, Doctor Mindyourmanners will have to find you too.

What would your manners machine look like?

THE END

CPSIA information can be obtained
at www.ICGtesting.com
Printed in the USA
LVHW071444251121
704431LV00020B/32